CORE LIBRARY OF US STATES

MONTANA

BY JANE VERNON

CONTENT CONSULTANT
Debra Mitchell
Program Specialist
Montana Historical Society
Outreach and Interpretation

Core Library

An Imprint of Abdo Publishing
abdobooks.com

abdobooks.com

Published by Abdo Publishing, a division of ABDO, PO Box 398166, Minneapolis, Minnesota 55439.

Printed in the United States of America, North Mankato, Minnesota.
052022
092022

THIS BOOK CONTAINS RECYCLED MATERIALS

Cover Photo: Shutterstock Images
Interior Photos: Tracy Hart/Shutterstock Images, 4–5; Red Line Editorial, 7 (Montana), 7 (USA); Pavel Tvrdy/Shutterstock Images, 10–11; Lewis and Clark Meeting Indians at Ross' Hole/Charles M. Russell/Oil on Canvas, 1912/Mural in State of Montana Capitol/Montana Historical Society Collection, X1912.06.01/Photograph by Don Beatty, 1999, 13; Mihai Andritoiu/Shutterstock Images, 15, 43; Shutterstock Images, 18 (flag); Scott E. Read/Shutterstock Images, 18 (bear); David Spates/Shutterstock Images, 18 (bird); Frank L. Jr./Shutterstock Images, 18 (flower); Dominic Gentilcore, PhD/Shutterstock Images, 18 (tree); iStockphoto, 20–21, 45; Matthieu Gallet/Shutterstock Images, 23; Amy Hyfield/US Forest Service/AP Images, 26; Brett French/The Billings Gazette/AP Images, 28–29; Danita Delimont/Shutterstock Images, 32; Ian MacNicol/Getty Images Sport/Getty Images, 34–35; Griffen Smith/The Billings Gazette/AP Images, 37; Timothy Yue/Shutterstock Images, 39

Editor: Angela Lim
Series Designer: Joshua Olson

Library of Congress Control Number: 2021951408

Publisher's Cataloging-in-Publication Data

Names: Vernon, Jane, author.
Title: Montana / by Jane Vernon
Description: Minneapolis, Minnesota : Abdo Publishing, 2023 | Series: Core library of US states | Includes online resources and index.
Identifiers: ISBN 9781532197673 (lib. bdg.) | ISBN 9781098270438 (ebook)
Subjects: LCSH: U.S. states--Juvenile literature. | Western States (U.S.)--Juvenile literature. | Montana--History--Juvenile literature. | Physical geography--United States--Juvenile literature.
Classification: DDC 978.6--dc23

Population demographics broken down by race and ethnicity come from the 2019 census estimate. Population totals come from the 2020 census.

CONTENTS

HOTEL MEADE

CHAPTER ONE

THE TREASURE STATE

A group of people including John White discovered gold in Bannack, Montana, in 1862. This was the first major gold discovery in the Montana region. Many miners rushed to the area to find gold. Bannack became the capital city of the Montana Territory.

Today the buildings from the gold rush are abandoned. Bannack State Park preserves the ghost town. Visitors can see the original buildings that housed the miners who came to

Hotel Meade in Bannack State Park has been closed since the 1940s.

PERSPECTIVES

BIG SKY COUNTRY

In 1967 the Montana State Highway Department began using "Big Sky Country" on Montana license plates. The state does not have many tall buildings that block the horizon. This allows people to see far off into the distance, making the amount of visible sky bigger than in more-populated areas. Author Christopher Paolini lives in Montana. He wrote about the state, "Everything is so big—the sky, the mountains, the windswept flatlands—it sinks into you, it shapes your body and your dreams."

pan for gold. Workers at the assay office weighed and valued gold. The assay office is one of more than 60 remaining structures at Bannack State Park.

Historic discoveries of gold and silver deposits gave rise to the state's nickname the Treasure State. Montana is also known for its beautiful skyline and many mountains.

ABOUT MONTANA

Montana is part of the northwestern United States. It shares borders with four other states. Idaho borders Montana to the west and south. Wyoming makes the

MAP OF MONTANA

Montana landscapes are major parts of the state's tourism. How does this map show you what Montana has to offer?

TRIPLE DIVIDE

A continental divide is when a change in elevation causes rivers to flow into different large bodies of water, such as the Pacific and Atlantic Oceans. Triple Divide Peak is a mountain peak in Glacier National Park. It is a three-way continental divide, which is rare. Water from the peak flows into the Atlantic Ocean, the Pacific Ocean, and also the Arctic Ocean through Hudson Bay. Over billions of years, plants and animals have moved upstream onto the peak. It now has one of the most diverse groups of plants and animals in North America.

rest of the state's southern border. North Dakota and South Dakota lie to the east. Canada forms Montana's northern border.

Montana is the fourth-largest US state in area, but it is not densely populated. Much of Montana is rural. In recent years, more people have been leaving the rural areas of Montana and moving to the cities. This is making the rural regions of Montana even more sparsely populated. Just over 100,000 people live in Billings, Montana's most populated city. Other major towns include Missoula,

Great Falls, and Bozeman. Smaller towns include Whitefish and Miles City. Helena became the capital of the Montana Territory in 1875 and is still the capital city today.

The towns have much to offer, but Montana is best known for its natural beauty. Grasslands and prairies lie in the east. The Rocky Mountains stretch across the western side of the state. Forests cover much of the state, and rivers wind through Montana. This includes the Roe River. At just 201 feet (61 m), it is the shortest river in the world. Adventure lovers enjoy skiing, white water rafting, and rock climbing.

Montana's state and national parks showcase its scenery. The northern and western entrances to Yellowstone National Park are located in Montana. Glacier National Park is in the northern part of the state. From growing towns to outdoor adventures, the Treasure State has something for everyone to enjoy.

CHAPTER TWO

HISTORY OF MONTANA

People have lived in what is now Montana for more than 12,000 years. When Europeans arrived in the region in the 1700s, many American Indian nations were already established there. Europeans traded tools and guns with American Indians, including the Blackfeet, in the Great Plains region. Horses and guns from French traders made hunting easier for the Blackfeet and

The Blackfeet Indian Memorial stands within Glacier National Park. The Blackfeet Indian reservation shares a border with the park.

other peoples. These goods also led to an increase in warfare between nations in the area.

European traders and explorers also spread new diseases to the American Indian people they came into contact with. These diseases, including smallpox and measles, killed many American Indians. The Salish had lived in the western Montana region for thousands of years. Historians estimate that diseases killed as much as 75 percent of the Salish peoples in the late 1700s.

MONTANA IN THE 1800s

In 1803 the US Congress bought a large area of land from France called the Louisiana Territory. It included present-day Montana. Meriwether Lewis and William Clark led an expedition to the western region, hoping to find a waterway that would connect the eastern United States with the Pacific Ocean. The crew arrived in Montana in 1805. Clark mapped the region and marked areas that could be sites for trading posts. People from several American Indian nations helped Lewis and Clark

A depiction of the Salish meeting with Lewis and Clark hangs in the Montana State Capitol.

along their journey. For example the Salish peoples gave the explorers horses that allowed them to cross the Bitterroot Mountains. This mountain range lies between present-day Montana and Idaho.

Soon after the Lewis and Clark expedition, US traders began arriving in the region. They set up trading forts to exchange beaver furs. The first trading post in Montana was established in 1807 along the Bighorn and Yellowstone Rivers. Rivers in the region, including the Missouri River, were important for transporting furs to other trading posts. The fur trade declined in the 1840s as beaver furs became less fashionable.

In 1848 gold was discovered in California. Many people crossed through Montana as they traveled west. The US government forced American Indian nations to sign treaties that would protect the American settlers. The treaties disrupted the lifestyles of many American Indian peoples. In 1855 nations in western Montana signed the Hellgate Treaty. The treaty forced the Bitterroot Salish, the Kalispel, and the Kootenai to give their land to US settlers. They had to move onto a reservation. Communication between the nations and the US government was poor. The US government provided poor translation. As a result the American Indian nations did not understand the full extent of the treaty.

When John White discovered gold in Montana in 1862, a wave of settlers entered the region. They formed Montana's first permanent settlement.

Helena first started as a mining town in 1864. Today the capital city is home to more than 33,000 people.

Montana was a part of the Idaho Territory at the time. More than 2,000 miners moved to Bannack in the year that followed John White's discovery. Miners discovered more gold at Last Chance Gulch in 1864. The town that grew around the site was Helena. The growing population led to the creation of the Montana Territory on May 26, 1864. Silver mining boomed in 1874, bringing even more people into the territory.

The population booms created more tensions between American settlers and American Indian peoples. Miners and settlers wanted the land for themselves. The US government tried to force American Indian nations to give up their lands and move to reservations. This led to the Great Sioux War (1876–1877). Lakota leaders Sitting Bull and Crazy Horse refused to sign treaties. The Northern Cheyenne also fought to protect their land. The Battle of the Little Bighorn was one of the most famous battles during the Great Sioux War. In 1876 the Lakota and Cheyenne defeated the US Army at this Montana site. But the

BEAR RIVER MASSACRE

In January 1870 the US Army attacked members of the Blackfeet Nation who were camping beside the Bear River. The army was seeking revenge against a Blackfeet man who had killed a white settler. But the army attacked the wrong camp. The US Army killed more than 200 Blackfeet people during the event known as the Bear River Massacre. In addition the army destroyed Blackfeet homes and supplies. Many of the Blackfeet men were away hunting during the time of the attack. Most of the Blackfeet people killed were elders, women, and children.

victory was short-lived. The US government increased its army presence in the region. Troops forced the Lakota and Cheyenne onto reservations.

PERSPECTIVES

SITTING BULL

Sitting Bull was a Lakota leader during the Battle of the Little Bighorn. He wanted to keep the Lakota people independent from white settlers. He wanted to maintain the Lakota lifestyle. Sitting Bull and other Lakota people refused to move onto a reservation. He said, "I have seen nothing that the white man has . . . which is as good as our right to roam and live on the open plains as we choose."

STATEHOOD AND GOVERNMENT

Montana's growing population led the territory to become the forty-first US state on November 8, 1889. Residents discussed important issues. For example women throughout Montana campaigned for the right to vote. Jeannette Rankin was one of the most famous leaders of the movement. In 1914 white women in Montana won the right to vote. This did not become

MONTANA QUICK FACTS

Take a close look at Montana's state flag and state symbols. What do they show you about Montana's geography and economy?

Abbreviation: MT
Nickname: The Treasure State
Motto: *Oro y plata* (Gold and silver)
Date of statehood: November 8, 1889
Capital: Helena
Population: 1,084,225
Area: 147,040 square miles (380,832 sq km)

STATE SYMBOLS

State animal
Grizzly bear

State flower
Bitterroot

State bird
Western meadowlark

State tree
Ponderosa pine

a national right until 1920. Montana voters elected Rankin to the US House of Representatives in 1916. She became the first female member of Congress.

Montana's government today has three branches. Officials in the legislative branch work to create laws. The executive branch includes the governor. Governors have the power to make laws official. The judicial branch is made up of the system of courts in Montana. There are eight federally recognized American Indian tribes in the state. Each has its own government.

FURTHER EVIDENCE

Chapter Two describes treaties that American Indian nations made with the US government. What was one of the main points about this topic? What evidence is included to support this point? Read the article at the website below. Does the information on the website support the main points of the chapter? Does it present new evidence?

HISTORY: THE EVOLUTION OF INDIAN TERRITORIES IN MONTANA

abdocorelibrary.com/montana

CHAPTER THREE

GEOGRAPHY AND CLIMATE

The western part of Montana is mountainous. The Rocky Mountains run from south-central Montana to the northwestern part of the state. Granite Peak is the tallest mountain peak in Montana. It has an elevation of 12,799 feet (3,901 m).

The Rocky Mountains divide eastern and western Montana. Flathead Lake sits in the Rocky Mountains. It is the largest natural freshwater lake in the western United States.

Grinnell Lake is one of many glacier-fed lakes at Glacier National Park.

GRIZZLY BEARS

Grizzly bears are Montana's state animal. These large mammals grow up to 8 feet (2 m) tall. They may weigh 900 pounds (410 kg). Grizzlies do not climb trees often because they are too big. However they can run up to 30 miles per hour (48 km/h). Grizzlies dig dens and hibernate through the winter. These bears can be quite aggressive. Female bears with cubs can be especially dangerous to people.

Glacier National Park is located in the Rocky Mountains in the northern region of Montana. Bitterroot flowers bloom along the foothills of the mountains. The park has a large population of grizzly bears. It is home to many other types of wildlife, such as bighorn sheep, elk, and small rodents called pikas. Approximately 276 types of birds live in Glacier National Park, and the park's waters host many types of fish. The park is most famous for its glaciers. Visitors can hike in the mountains to see these huge ice sheets.

Glaciers played an important role in the formation of Montana's Great Plains, which are in the eastern part

The pronghorn is the fastest land mammal in North America. It can reach speeds of 60 miles per hour (97 km/h).

of the state. The glaciers pressed down on the region for millions of years. They deposited fertile soils as they moved. Today the soil has given rise to many types of grasses.

Montana has one of the largest native grasslands in the United States. The Great Plains are home to Montana's state bird, the western meadowlark. Rare birds, including burrowing owls and mountain plovers, also live in the plains. The pronghorn is a type of antelope. It migrates across Montana and the Great

Plains each year. It travels more than 500 miles (805 km) during its migration.

Approximately 25 percent of Montana is forested. Eastern and western forests are made up of different types of trees. In eastern Montana, ponderosa pines dominate the forests. This type of tree is Montana's state tree. Lodgepole pines and Douglas firs are major trees in western forests.

CLIMATE

Climate varies between Montana's geographic regions. In general, eastern Montana experiences warmer summers and colder winters than western Montana. Less precipitation falls on the Great Plains. Eastern Montana receives less than 15 inches (38 cm) of rain and snow every year.

Elevation affects the climate in western Montana. Higher elevations can become extremely cold. Montana has recorded some of the coldest temperatures in the United States. In 1954 the temperature near Helena plummeted to −70 degrees Fahrenheit (−57°C). Higher elevations also receive more snowfall than lower elevations. Climate scientists estimate that some mountain peaks receive approximately 250 inches (635 cm) of snow each winter. Meanwhile the western valleys do not typically get more than 70 inches (178 cm) of snow.

In addition to heavy snowfall, Montana is at risk for wildfires. Lightning strikes can ignite dry forest areas. But people are responsible

PERSPECTIVES

DISAPPEARING GLACIERS

When Glacier National Park was founded in 1910, it was home to 150 glaciers. Today fewer than 30 glaciers remain in the park. Climate experts predict that there may be no glaciers left in the park by 2030. Although glaciers are melting all over the world due to climate change, that warming is happening faster in western Montana than in other places. Montana temperatures have increased at almost double the global average. US Geological Survey researcher Dan Fagre says, "We're an early indicator of the kinds of changes that are going to occur elsewhere."

Many wildfires blazed across Montana in June 2021, including the Robertson Draw Fire near Red Lodge.

for approximately 60 percent of Montana's wildfires. They may accidentally cause wildfires when they do not properly extinguish campfires. Wildfires can damage landscapes and hurt wildlife. Breathing in smoke is harmful to human and animal health. But wildfires also maintain forests. They clear land and allow new types of plants to grow. These plants attract different types of animals. Lodgepole pines depend on fire. They drop cones that contain seeds. The cones open and expose the seeds only in extreme heat.

STRAIGHT TO THE SOURCE

Lewis and Clark entered into the Montana region in 1805. In the early 1800s, there weren't official spellings for words in the United States. Lewis described the geography in a journal entry:

> *The hills and river Clifts which we passed today exhibit a most romantic appearance. The bluffs of the river rise to the hight of from 2 to 300 feet (0.6–91 m). . . . They are formed of remarkable white sandstone which is sufficiently soft. . . . The water in the course of time in decending from those hills and plains on either side of the river has trickled down the soft sand clifts and [worn] it into a thousand [strange] figures, which with the help of a little imagination . . . are made to represent eligant ranges of lofty freestone buildings.*

Source: Meriwether Lewis. "May 31, 1805." *Journals of the Lewis & Clark Expedition*, n.d., lewisandclarkjournals.unl.edu. Accessed 9 July 2021.

CONSIDER YOUR AUDIENCE

Review this passage closely. Consider how you would adapt it for your younger friends or siblings. Rewrite the passage so that they can understand it. What is the best way to get your point across to this audience? How is your writing different from the original text, and why?

CHAPTER FOUR

RESOURCES AND ECONOMY

The energy industry is an important part of Montana's economy. Some of the energy sources in the state are nonrenewable. These sources include coal and oil. Most of the state's oil is in the northeastern region along the border with North Dakota. More than 30 percent of US coal comes from Montana.

Nearly half of Montana's electricity comes from renewable resources, such as water and wind. Hydroelectricity accounts for 40 percent

Powerhouses stand beside Fort Peck Lake. The lake is the largest body of water in Montana.

of the state's electricity needs. The Fort Peck Dam is a major hydroelectric dam that crosses the Missouri River. In addition to providing energy for the state, the Fort Peck Dam is an important tourist location. The dam creates Fort Peck Lake, where people enjoy nature trails and outdoor activities.

Companies place wind turbines across the open Great Plains region. Wind energy provides 7.5 percent of the state's renewable energy. Experts predict that Montana's wind energy production will increase. They expect wind to provide more energy in the state than coal does by 2040.

The land in Montana is also rich in metals and minerals.

THE RISE OF THE RANCHES

The US Congress passed the Enlarged Homestead Act in 1909. It encouraged farmers to take up large areas of land in Montana. After maintaining a homestead for three years, a farmer would own it. This motivated US settlers from other areas to come to Montana and start ranches to raise beef and grow wheat.

Gold, silver, and copper deposits drew people to the state. Montana has two official gemstones, sapphire and agate. Both can be found in the state. People still mine for precious rocks and metals, but these are no longer a leading source of revenue. Montana is the leading US producer of talc, a mineral used in cosmetics.

PERSPECTIVES

MONTANA TIMBER INDUSTRY

Montana's timber industry began to decline in the 1980s. Some blame the decline on environmental regulations. Scientist George Wuerthner says the timber industry has moved to the southeastern United States. He believes states in the Southeast are better suited for wood production than Montana is. It takes 60 to 100 years to grow a tree that is 12 inches (30 cm) thick in Montana. A tree can grow to the same size in Georgia or Mississippi in just 10 years. The southeastern climate allows trees to grow more quickly.

AGRICULTURE AND FORESTRY

Besides mining and energy production, agriculture makes up a large part of Montana's economy.

Montana is home to more than 2.5 million cattle.

Farms and ranches cover approximately 59.7 million acres (24.2 million ha) of Montana. Wheat and cattle are the top products. Together they make up 75 percent of Montana's agricultural income. Farmers also grow cherries, sugar beets, potatoes, and hay. Montana ranks second in the United States for honey production. Agriculture brings about $5.2 billion to the state's economy each year.

Timber is another important industry in Montana, though today the state produces much less than it did in the past. The industry peaked in the 1960s and 1980s. In an effort to protect Montana's forest habitats, the state and federal governments purchased more than 500,000 acres (202,000 ha) of forest that was once used for timber.

More than 10 percent of Montana jobs are related to tourism and recreation. People working in these jobs take care of tourists. They may work in hotels or restaurants. Some work at Montana's national parks. Glacier National Park is one popular tourist attraction. Big Sky Resort is a well-known place to ski.

EXPLORE ONLINE

Chapter Four touches on some of the livestock and crops that farmers in Montana produce. The article at the website below goes into more depth on the state's agriculture. What information from the article backs up what you read in Chapter Four? What additional information did you learn about agriculture in Montana from the article?

AGRICULTURE AND BUSINESS

abdocorelibrary.com/montana

PyeongChang 2018
14

CHAPTER FIVE

PEOPLE AND PLACES

Montana was home to more than 1 million people in 2021. Most of the population is white. American Indians make up more than 6 percent of the population. Approximately 4 percent of the population is Hispanic or Latino. Asian and Black people each make up less than 1 percent of Montana's population.

Montana's beautiful mountains and abundant winter snowfall make it an ideal place for winter sports. Two notable Winter

Darian Stevens competes in the freestyle skiing event during the 2018 Pyeongchang Olympics in South Korea.

ELLA HASKELL

Ella Knowles Haskell graduated from college in Maine and studied law in New Hampshire. She moved to Helena in 1888. But women were not allowed to be attorneys in Montana at the time. Haskell worked to pass a bill that gave women the right to practice law. She succeeded in 1889 and became the first female lawyer in Montana.

Olympics athletes grew up skiing in Montana. Maggie Voisin is a skier. She was chosen to compete in the women's slopestyle event at the 2014 Winter Olympics in Sochi, Russia. Another Montanan, Darian Stevens, is a freestyle skier. She competed in the 2018 Winter Olympics in Pyeongchang, South Korea. She came in seventeenth in women's ski slopestyle.

ATTRACTIONS AND EVENTS

Montanans celebrate cultures at the Festival of the Nations. This two-day gathering is the oldest cultural festival in the state. Lifestyles and customs from Ireland, Italy, Germany, and other European nations are

People from the Crow Tribe reenacted the Battle of the Little Bighorn during the 2021 Crow Native Days.

celebrated at the event. People from these countries played an important role in Montana's mining history.

Crow Native Days on the Crow Reservation is another cultural celebration. Montanans and visitors can learn about American Indian heritage in Montana. The Crow Tribe also hosts a rodeo and athletic competitions.

PERSPECTIVES

NOT BACKING DOWN

Elouise Pepion Cobell was a member of the Blackfeet Nation. In 1996 she filed one of the largest lawsuits ever filed against the US government. She said the government had misused funds that were supposed to be for American Indian reservations. The people living on these reservations were not getting the resources they were owed. In 2009 a decision was finally made. Cobell won the case. The US government paid $3.4 billion to American Indian nations.

Montana's tourism department advertises the state as Big Sky Country. Many people come to visit Montana's 55 state parks. These parks give visitors a look into Montana's geography and settlement. The National Park Service protects ten locations throughout the state. This includes a long section of the Lewis and Clark National Historic Trail. Hikers can retrace the route the Lewis and Clark expedition took. Visitors can trek through national forests, which cover some 10 million acres (4 million ha).

Whitefish Mountain Resort is one of the largest ski resorts in the United States.

During the winter, skiers can enjoy snowy views from the slopes and the hundreds of miles of trails.

Large cities, such as Billings, Missoula, and Bozeman, have museums and cultural centers. Historic mining towns, such as the Richest Hill on Earth in Butte, are now museums. Visitors can see original buildings from the 1800s and learn about the history of mining. The Western Heritage Center in Billings was built in 1901. It houses 17,000 artifacts from Montana history. In Great Falls, visitors can learn about the famed US artist Charles M. Russell, known as the Cowboy Artist, at the C. M. Russell Museum.

Montana draws people who love outdoor adventures. They can revisit history. They can ski, hike, or fish. They can relax and enjoy the big sky. Natural resources first attracted people to the Treasure State. Today many people who live in Montana enjoy the great outdoors and all the state has to offer.

STRAIGHT TO THE SOURCE

The Montana Office of Tourism encourages travelers to visit year-round. But the fall can be a great time to visit the state. In a press release, the tourism department shared:

> *Montana is a place you have to see to believe, and autumn in the Treasure State is no exception. With fewer crowds in the fall, it's almost like you have the place to yourself. Combined with the crisp autumn air, pleasant daytime temperatures and the changing colors of fall, it's no surprise that this time of year is perfect for experiencing the Big Sky state. One of the best ways to discover Montana is hiking. With over 15,000 miles (24,000 km) of trails ready to be explored, Montana is a hiker's paradise. Discover all the unspoiled beauty this state has to offer and bask in the red and gold hues around every bend.*

Source: "Discover Montana's Golden Season." *Montana Office of Tourism*, 2020, visitmt.com. Accessed 20 July 2021.

WHAT'S THE BIG IDEA?

Take a close look at this article. What is the main connection being made between the fall and Montana's landscape? What about the season makes it a great time to visit the state?

IMPORTANT DATES

12,000 years ago
Humans first enter the Montana region.

1805
Meriwether Lewis and William Clark enter Montana as they journey through new land from the Louisiana Purchase.

1807
Montana's first trading post is established along the Bighorn and Yellowstone Rivers.

1855
The Bitterroot Salish, the Kalispel, and the Kootenai sign the Hellgate Treaty. The treaty forces them to give their homelands to US settlers and move onto reservations.

1862
John White and others discover gold in Montana, setting off a rush of settlers into the region.

1876
The Lakota and the Cheyenne defeat the US Army at the Little Bighorn.

1889
Montana becomes the forty-first state on November 8.

1914
White Montana women win the right to vote.

1916
Montana voters elect Jeannette Rankin to the US House of Representatives. Rankin becomes the first female member of Congress.

2009
Elouise Pepion Cobell wins her lawsuit on behalf of American Indian nations against the US government.

STOP AND THINK

Why Do I Care?

Maybe you haven't visited Glacier National Park. But that doesn't mean you can't think about how climate change affects the park. How does climate change affect glaciers and wildlife? How does a changing climate affect history, resources, and people?

Surprise Me

Chapter Four describes Montana's energy industry. After reading about Montana's energy production, what two or three facts did you find most surprising? Write a few sentences about each fact. Why did you find each fact surprising?

Tell the Tale

Chapter Two discusses the discovery of gold and silver in Montana. Imagine you were a gold miner who came to the region in the 1860s. Write 200 words about your experience. What buildings did you find in the mining town? What services were available?

Another View

This book talks about the Battle of the Little Bighorn. As you know, every source is different. Ask a librarian or another adult to help you find another source about the Battle of the Little Bighorn. Write a short essay comparing and contrasting the new source's point of view with that of this book's author. What is the point of view of each author? How are they similar and why? How are they different and why?

GLOSSARY

assay office
a government or company office where workers assess the value of precious metals

deposit
a natural source of a resource or metal

fertile
rich in nutrients for growing plants

fund
money that is saved or given for a specific purpose

hydroelectric
electricity generated from flowing water

mineral
a nonliving substance found naturally on Earth

native
naturally occurring in a region

nonrenewable
at risk of being used up

revenue
income from the sales or services of an industry, a company, or an individual

rural
having to do with the countryside

ONLINE RESOURCES

To learn more about Montana, visit our free resource websites below.

Core Library CONNECTION
FREE! COMMON CORE MULTIMEDIA RESOURCES

Visit **abdocorelibrary.com** or scan this QR code for free Common Core resources for teachers and students, including vetted activities, multimedia, and booklinks, for deeper subject comprehension.

Booklinks NONFICTION NETWORK
FREE! ONLINE NONFICTION RESOURCES

Visit **abdobooklinks.com** or scan this QR code for free additional online weblinks for further learning. These links are routinely monitored and updated to provide the most current information available.

LEARN MORE

Horowitz, Ellen. *What I Saw in Glacier: A Kid's Guide to the National Park*. Riverbend, 2017.

Lawrence, Blythe. *The Lewis and Clark Expedition*. Weigl, 2020.

INDEX

About the Author

Jane Vernon is the author of more than 100 books for children, both nonfiction and fiction. Her favorite topics are nature; arts and crafts; food and cooking; biographies; health; survival; and science, technology, engineering, and math (STEM). Jane and her husband live on the central coast of California.